NOR: PP

GW00715588

his bo
ma

30130 144593182

CHOICE

A Satirical Comedy

PETER HORSLER

SAMUEL FRENCH

FRENCH

LONDON
NEW YORK TORONTO SYDNEY HOLLYWOOD

Please note our NEW ADDRESS:

Samuel French Ltd
52 Fitzroy Street London W1P 6JR
Tel: 01 - 387 9373

CHARACTERS

First Lady
Second Lady } Residents of the "People's Rest Centre",
Third Lady } all in their mid-seventies
Mother, a mother of the mid-nineteen-seventies (D)
Child, her thirteen-year-old daughter (D)
Shop Assistant (D)
Television Director (D)
Cameraman (D)
First Actress: Fairy Godmother (D)
Second Actress: Cinderella (D)
Head of Advertising
Shop Steward
Managing Director (D)
Principal Shareholder
Second Shareholder (D)
New Managing Director, Miss Ruth Less
Monique, designer
A Model (D)
Doctor (Medical Officer)
Minister of Health

The play can be cast for 8 men and 12 women; it can also be played by an all-women cast. The parts marked (D) can be doubled if desired

The action takes place in the Day Room of the "People's Rest Centre"

Time—the year 2040

CHOICE

The Day Room of the "People's Rest Centre" in the year 2040

The CURTAIN *rises on a bare curtain set, except for six futuristic chairs. Three of these are set up* R, *three down* L. *The two chairs farthest up* R *are occupied by the Second and Third Ladies. The First Lady is down* RC, *looking out front, as if through a window*

First Lady Look, girls, it's not so bad after all, rather quaint really.

Second Lady Come and sit down, dear, you'll have backache again.

First Lady They've laid it out with concrete, paving slabs and pre-cast blocks. It's like being transplanted back to the seventies.

Third Lady (*hobbling down to her*) I shouldn't really. I'm supposed to keep off my feet, but you make it sound so idyllic.

First Lady They've caught the atmosphere somehow, makes me feel quite nostalgic.

Second Lady Come away, the pair of you! You've no cause to long for the seventies. That's when our troubles began.

First Lady (*feeling her back*) You're right, dear. I should sit and rest.

Third Lady (*taking her arm and moving* C) I'll help you, dear; we make one perfect specimen between us: my good back and your good feet.

First Lady Pity we can't have a rejuvenation certificate between us—it would be twenty extra years apiece.

Second Lady Not in the twenty-forties you can't. It's not nineteen-eighty now you know, with a liberal, democratic government.

The First and Third Ladies sit

Third Lady Has anyone ever tried to petition the Grand Master?

First Lady (*looking around*) Shush, dear!

Second Lady It's all right, they're not interested in us any more.

Third Lady No, we're written off; put out to grass. When I think of Margaret Tanner and Joan Gifford, both playing tennis again by now I shouldn't wonder. I'm as fit as they are. What do weak ankles matter? I wasn't born with them. It's not as if it's hereditary or anything.

First Lady It's the rules, dear, you can't have a rejuvenation certificate if you have any sort of deformity. They say the process won't rectify damage; only make it worse.

Second Lady And who makes the rules, the Prime Committee: I bet they've all got certificates.

Third Lady Well it won't help us if they have. Once you're in a people's rest home, you only leave it one way.

First Lady It's very comfortable here. I don't know that I want to live to a hundred-and-thirty, not with my back anyway.

Second Lady And who's to blame for your back, my bunions and her ankles? If we'd been stopped from wearing stupid shoes in our teens, we could all be playing tennis again and looking forward to the next sixty years.

First Lady I never liked tennis, anyway, but I know what you mean.

Third Lady I know who was to blame in my case, my mother. She was too indulgent, by far.

The Mother and Child enter up L

She should have said no, insisted on me wearing sensible shoes.

Child Not this shop, Mum, they only sell old granny shoes.

Mother (*dragging her into the room*) Don't you start again, my girl! For the last time, you'll have a sensible pair or none at all.

Child You just don't care; you don't care if they laugh at me! You're so square, so stuck up. My friends' mums understand—not like you.

A Shop Assistant enters down R

Shop Assistant Can I help you, madam?

Mother Yes, I want a pair of black, school shoes. Not too expensive.

The Child takes a pose

Shop Assistant With flat heels, madam?

Child Shan't wear them, you'll waste your money.

Mother (*to her daughter*) You show off and I'll tell your father!

Child More sensible than you; he'd understand. I wish he'd come.

Mother (*to the Shop Assistant*) Perhaps a small heel. They're so difficult at this age, aren't they?

Shop Assistant They grow up so quickly. We have just the thing. Would a five be about right?

Mother (*indicating her daughter's shoes*) Those are a four-and-a-half, but they're a bit tight. We'll try a five.

Shop Assistant Won't keep you a moment, madam.

The Shop Assistant exits down R

The Child runs after the Shop Assistant as if to stop her, then turns to the Mother

Child Why've I got to have granny shoes? They'll all be in fashionable shoes.

Mother I'm not going through that again!

Child Don't want me to be happy do you? You don't know what it's like. Bet your mother wasn't hard like you. Bet she didn't go on. (*Crying and moving away*) You hate me, that's what, hate me.

Mother (*following her*) Stop it! Do you hear, stop it! I'm not putting up with it—not another scene like the last one. If you're so stupid you want to be a cripple at my age . . .

Child (*sobbing*) You're just saying that 'cause you want me to look stupid!

Mother I just hope when you grow up; I just hope you have a daughter and . . .

Child I shall let her buy her own shoes. Shall have more feeling than you.

Mother (*fumbling for her purse*) Right, I've had all I can take. Don't you ever say I didn't try, that's all. Here, take this. (*She thrusts three five-pound notes into the Child's hand*) Go on, get whatever you want. Ruin your feet if you want but don't blame me, that's all, don't blame me!

The Child rushes out up L, *followed by the Mother. The Shop Assistant returns with several boxes of shoes*

Shop Assistant They've gone! Some people have no patience these days, no patience at all.

Third Lady (*standing*) Why couldn't you have been quicker? If you'd hurried up a bit I might never have started buying my own shoes.

Shop Assistant Really, madam, I don't see how I can be held
responsible. You were a very wayward child as I recall.

The Shop Assistant exits down R

Second Lady (*pulling her down*) It wasn't her fault or your
mother's. It was advertising that did it. They conned us into
everything. They set the fahion; told us what we should wear.
We were only impressionable kids.

Television Director (*off*) Hurry it up now. This will be the final
take.

The Television Director enters up L *and crosses down* R. *He is
carrying a clapperboard. Behind him is a Cameraman, wearing
earphones and carrying a camera and tripod. Following are two
Actresses, one dressed as Cinderella in her ball gown, the other
as the Fairy Godmother*

It we don't get it this time, there'll be hell to pay! Hurry up
with that camera. Beginning positions, please, girls!

The Cameraman sets up the camera down L *and the Actresses
position themselves up* C. *The Fairy Godmother stands up* L *of
Cinders with her wand raised. Cinders looks down at her own
silver slippers*

That's it. Ready on camera? Right?

The Cameraman nods

Right, darlings, let's go for a sweet take. (*He darts forward and
holds the clapperboard in front of the camera*) Run camera!

Cameraman Camera running.

Television Director *Withit Shoe Company* commercial, take
fifteen. (*He dashes down* RC) Action!

Fairy Godmother (*waving her wand*)
        There, now all is done.
        Away to the ball, my child, have fun.
        But remember, do not get too tight;
        You must away by midnight.

Cinderella (*waggling her left foot to the Fairy Godmother*)
        I'm not going, Fairy G.,
        Not in these old silver slippers,
        They're real old granny shoes.
        I'd rather wear a pair of kippers.

Fairy Godmother Hush, my child, allay your fears

She produces a pair of shoes with semi-spherical soles from the inside of her cloak

> I've brought a pair of *Semi-Spheres.*

Cinderella (*taking them*)

> Oh, how lovely, Fairy G.

Crossing in front of her

> Now the prince will look at me

Turning to the Fairy Godmother

> I'm sorry to stop and talk

Holding up the shoes

> But how in these shall I walk?

Fairy Godmother It's simple, dear, for all to see

She opens her cloak to reveal a small pair of crutches

> With every pair these come free.

Cinderella (*kissing her*)

> I love you, love you, Fairy G.,
> For being kind to little me.
> This night of you shall I think
> And bring you back a whopping drink.

Fairy Godmother No, dear, do not thank me with your booze,
All thanks is due to *Withit Shoes.*

They both smile into the camera, holding out the shoes and displaying the crutches

Television Director Cut! Very nice girls. (*To the Cameraman*) Was sound all right?

The Cameraman nods

That's fine then. Take a break, girls.

The Actresses and Cameraman exit up L

The Television Director stays for a moment, checking through his shooting schedule

Second Lady (*hobbling down to the Television Director*) You should be thoroughly ashamed, trying to hoodwink youngsters into buying such rubbish! Haven't you any conscience? Don't you give a thought to the damage you might be doing?

Television Director I beg your pardon, madam?

Second Lady Encouraging impressionable kids to break their ankles or their necks! How can you do it?

Television Director It's not up to me, madam, to decide what is to be advertised. I'm presented with a script and I have to direct it, that's all. If you have any complaints, I suggest you write to our company.

The Head of Advertising enters up L

Head of Advertising (*coming to the Television Director*) The schedule's a day behind, surely you've completed the *Withit* contract. (*He sees the Second Lady*) Who is this person?

Television Director A member of the public. She's complaining that our advertising is irresponsible.

Head of Advertising Is she, indeed. Well madam, let me tell you that if we started criticizing the products of our clients, we should very quickly be out of business and that would mean a great deal more unemployment that there is at present.

Second Lady Somebody should do something, that's what I'm saying.

Head of Advertising Then you'd better say it to the manufacturers. It has nothing to do with us. (*Moving away*) Come, Hargreaves, I want to go over tomorrow's shooting.

Television Director (*following*) The airgun project? Fancy blaming us for *Semi-Spheres*.

First Lady (*pulling the Second Lady back to her seat*) Come and sit down, dear, it's no good getting yourself in a state. I'm sure she's right.

Second Lady (*limping back to her seat*) I'm not just thinking of my bunions. It's the principle. (*She sits*) They should use their powers of persuasion responsibly.

Third Lady She's probably right: it's the maker's fault and I've been blaming mother all these years.

The Shop Steward enters up L *and rushes down to address the audience*

Shop Steward Brothers, I've convened this meeting 'cos of

rumours. There's bin talk of redundancies. You've 'eard it
same as I have. You're worried, same as me. But, brothers,
times is not what they was, times is different now. The old days
when we could be cast on the streets like so much unwanted
junk are gone. They can't throw us in the gutter when business
is bad and pick us out when it bucks up. And why can't they?
'Cos of the Union; 'cos now we speak wiv' one voice; act as
one. You've 'eard that business is bad, the order books empty.
What's the use then, you say, what's the use of strikin', when
there's no work to strike from? I'll tell yer, brothers: to 'it out
at management, that's what; to show they can't manage.
(*Moving* L *to address a small group*) You can shake your 'eads
but I tell yer: management is our boss but they 'ave bosses too.
(*To all the audience*) Yes, brothers, the shareholders are their
bosses and they won't want us out 'cos then there'll be no
business left to sell. So what should we do, shake our 'eads,
doff our caps and go quietly on the dole? No more we shouldn't,
not if we speak wiv' one voice: tell 'em why there ain't no
work, tell 'em our shoes don't sell 'cos they're out of date;
'cos management's got no vision and's out of touch wiv market
trends. It's not us should go, but management. (*Raising his
fist*) We'll have 'em fired 'fore they fire us. Don't worry
brothers, trust in the Union. We've set the wheels in motion,
started the ball rollin', put a spanner in the works. If management can't keep us in work, management will 'ave to go. It's
us what runs this factory; the sweat of our brows, the toil of
our bodies. They can't cast us off like an old coat, no more
they can't, 'cos we 'ave the Union. I'm off, now, brothers, to
negotiate. I'll put 'em in their place, don't you worry. (*Shaking
his fist*) They'll not take the bread out of our mouves no more!

The Shop Steward exits R. *Two white-coated Women, as if
nurses in the rest home, carry on a small table on which are some
papers. They place the table up* C *then fetch two chairs which they
place behind it. As they exit up* L, *the Managing Director enters
down* R, *moves to the table and sits. After arranging the papers,
the Managing Director stands and addresses the audience*

Managing Director Members of the Board, Shareholders of the
company, we ail know why this extra-ordinary meeting has

been called, so I will not waste time on preliminaries. In short,
I am being censored, pilloried, rejected, cast off. For thirty
years I have made huge profits for you all. You have been kept
in luxury by my efforts, enjoying the fruits of our society without lifting a finger. Throughout those years I could do no
wrong; my name was dropped in board rooms up and down
the country. I became a symbol for stability, a guarantee of
good faith, a blueprint for success. But in two short years of
falling orders and diminishing returns, suddenly my image is
changed—the gilt edges have worn off. Now I am a reactionary,
behind the times, lacking in vision; a fuddy-duddy who cannot
adapt to new trends. But those of you who say these things do
me an injustice. I am flexible in marketing, in business management, in the use of modern technology. I understand the need
for rationalization, of the redeployment of labour, the adapta-
tion of new materials, but I will not desert my principles of
good design, will not pander to the fickle tastes of a manipu-
lated public.

Principal Shareholder (*shouting from the auditorium*) You can't
sell people what they don't want!

Managing Director People are not fools. Once they know the
facts: if we can put over to them that fitness for purpose is the
first principle of design . . .

Second Shareholder (*shouting from the auditorium*) Rubbish! It's
not our job to educate the public.

Managing Director We have a moral responsibility to . . .

Principal Shareholder Your only responsibility is to make money.

Second Shareholder Hear! Hear!

Managing Director Surely, you are not advocating that we
imitate this cheap, foreign rubbish?

Second Shareholder It sells doesn't it?

Principal Shareholder The first principle of business is profit!

Managing Director Grotesque distortions of footwear, is that
what you want?

Second Shareholder It's what the customer wants!

Principal Shareholder We only serve the public!

Managing Director Have you no conscience concerning our
product?

Second Shareholder We don't force people to buy!

Principal Shareholder Let the buyer beware.

Managing Director Then, in that case, Ladies and Genetlemen, you leave me no alternative but to resign.

The Principle Shareholder climbs on to the stage

Whatever demands have been made of me over the years, I have done my best to meet. I have always been willing to comply with your wishes as long as I could believe in our product. But now . . .

Principal Shareholder Yes, yes, thank you. As Principal Shareholder I accept your resignation. Shareholders of the company, I am sure you share my feelings of sorrow and regret in hearing of the resignation of our chairman and managing director. I would ask you to show your appreciation of his long and devoted service but time is getting on and some of us have trains to catch.

The Managing Director exits sadly up L

Of course, I did not know that we would lose our esteemed chairman today, but intuition prompted me to bring a good friend of mine who would make an admirable replacement. I'm sure our ex-director—(*turning to the table*)—will not object—oh, he's gone, well never mind, it simplifies matters—if I introduce her to you. (*He beckons down* R)

Miss Less enters down R *and moves to the Principal Shareholder*

This is Miss Less. Ruth, my dear, welcome to the company. Fellow shareholders, of course it is not my place as principal shareholder to make new appointments, that must be a democratic procedure, but I would like you to listen to Miss Less's ideas on how the company might develop. (*Moving to the chair down* L *and indicating to Miss Less to speak*). Ruth, dear . . . (*He sits*)

Miss Less (*with a glance at the Principal Shareholder*) If the board should appoint me, I would suggest first that we change the name of the company. *Steadfast Shoes* does rather handicap our image from the outset. I would like to offer—the *Withit Shoe Company*. Secondly, if we are to live up to such a title, we shall need new designers. Naturally, I am not advocating wholesale sackings but there are some well-tried, cheap redundancy schemes available to us. We need to concentrate on the teenage

market, where the real money is, and to do that we need new
designs. Designs, ladies and gentlemen, that are radically
different. Teenagers are struggling to establish a separate
identity; they want to be different. It is our duty then to offer
a symbol of difference in the shoes that we create.

Principal Shareholder Hear, hear, we are the servants of the
teenagers.

Miss Less But perhaps I can illustrate more clearly what I mean
by demonstration. On the off-chance that you might be interested, I have brought along my chief designer. (*She beckons
down* R)

Monique enters down R *and crosses to the Principal Shareholder*

Monique has worked for me for the past five years and pro-
duced all of our best selling lines.

Monique (*in a phoney French accent*) Madame is too kind.

Miss Less It would not be an exaggeration to say that the company's success has been due to Monique.

Monique Madame is too kind.

Miss Less Now Monique, it's up to you (*She sits on the chair next
to the Principal Shareholder*)

Monique Ladies and gentlemen, with your language I am not so
good, but I would like—how you say—to demonstrate for you,
my latest creation—(*she claps her hands and looks down* R)—
which I have called *Loppies*.

*The Model enters and moves to Monique. She is wearing a shoe
on her left foot with a four-inch platform, and a flat-soled shoe
on her right. She leans at an angle of forty-five degrees as she
walks*

Months of hard work have gone into the design of this pair of
shoes. I wanted in the first place to create something different,
to get away from the conventional. (*To the Model*) Darling,
would you move around a little.

The Model hobbles in a circle

I wanted all wearers of *Loppies* to feel different, to stand out
so that they could identify with each other.

*Through the next part of the speech, the Model fits her pose to
Monique's words*

Here we have two women in one. If a lady's escort walks on her left, he feels that he is out with a different girl than if he walks on her right. And, as you English say: "variety is nice in life". A man walking with a girl in *Loppies* has, at one moment, a tall, aloof lady and, at the next, an intimate short lady. With *Loppies* you can be the leaning kind or the keep your distance kind.

Miss Less Well done, excellent.

Monique (*to the Model*) Thank you, darling.

The Model exits down R

Principal Shareholder (*to Miss Less*) Nothing short of brilliant, my dear, absolute magic.

Monique (*turning to Principal Shareholder*) You are too kind.

Miss Less (*moving to Monique*) Thank you, my dear, very powerfully presented. I'll be in touch.

Monique goes to exit R, *but is accosted by the Second Lady*

Second Lady Just a minute, just a minute, call yourself a designer? You should be horse-whipped!

Monique (*dropping her French accent*) Get out of the way, you old trout!

Principal Shareholder (*jumping up and rushing to the Second Lady*) This is a private meeting, madam! Who are you? Are you a shareholder?

Second Lady I'm a victim, that's what I am, one of your victims. (*Pointing at Monique*) She wanted us to be different. Well we are different: different from Margaret Tanner and Joan Gifford; so different that we can't take the rejuvenation programme.

Principal Shareholder She's mad. How did she get in here? (*To Monique*) I'm so sorry, my dear.

Monique (*again adopting her French accent*) You are too kind.

Principal Shareholder (*to the Second Lady*) Will you leave, madam, or do I have to have you ejected!

Second Lady All right, I'm going. It's too late now, anyway. (*She returns to her seat*)

Principal Shareholder What an incredible nerve, an ordinary member of the public in our meeting. They think because they buy our shoes that they can tell us how to run our business.

Monique They'll be telling me how to design next.

Principal Shareholder The idea! Sorry, my dear, I hope this little incident won't stop you from joining us.

Monique Have no fear, madame, Monique is not influenced by the general public in any way.

Principal Shareholder I should hope not. Well, we'll be in touch.

Monique Au revoir, madame.

Monique exits down R

Principal Shareholder (*returning to Miss Less*) Most regrettable, my dear, I hope you're not having second thoughts.

Miss Less I've never had to resort to thinking twice.

Principal Shareholder (*to the audience*) Ladies and gentlemen, I have been so impressed by Miss Less that I propose we vote her into the chair here and now in a truly democratic way. Those in favour of Miss Less as Managing Director, please raise your hands. (*Counting*) One, two, and with my casting vote of fifty-two per cent of the shares, that means my proposition is carried. (*To Miss Less, shaking her hand*) Congratulations, my dear, you are the new Managing Director of *Steadfast Shoes*.

Miss Less *Withit Shoes.*

Principal Shareholder Yes, yes, what a fast worker you are.

Miss Less As the new manager, I have to report that the board will meet in precisely five minutes time to discuss the promotion of the new Loppies. This meeting is closed.

Principal Shareholder Well done, well done, my capital is in good hands. We have just time for a quick sherry in the office.

Miss Less A scotch, in my office.

Principal Shareholder In your office, of course.

Miss Less and the Principal Shareholder exit up L

Second Lady How you two could sit there, saying nothing, I don't know.

Third Lady What can we do, the past is past.

Second Lady At least we know who's to blame.

First Lady Not really, dear, after all the old manager resigned rather than produce dreadful shoes. We just can't blame management, not as a whole that is.

Third Lady Shareholders, they're the worst.

Second Lady That new manager, she had a lot to answer for.

First Lady Anyone might be a shareholder. I am, I'm afraid.

Second Lady I blame the advertisers.
First Lady But they're only doing their job.
Third Lady It was so unbalanced.

The Doctor enters up L, *carrying a chart. He is followed by the Minister of Health. They sit at the table and converse quietly*

There should have been advertising against dangerous foot-wear, like they did for cigarettes.
First Lady Do you think we'd have listened, dear? I wonder.
Second Lady I don't think they were very serious about it.
Doctor (*standing and speaking to the audience*) Ladies and Gentle-men, how very gratifying that so many of you have turned out to hear our Minister speak this afternoon. It only goes to show just how seriously you take this threat to the nation's feet. Well, I won't keep you in suspense. As your Medical Officer, it is my proud privilege to introduce our Minister of Health who, of course, needs no introduction from me.

The Minister rises and the Doctor sits, clapping

Minister Thank you Doctor. (*Moving down to address the audience*) Ladies and Gentlemen, I know in addressing you this afternoon that I am preaching to the converted. That you share the government's concern for what is happening to the feet of the the people is not only evident from your presence but also from expressions on your faces. It is a measure of your govern-ment's concern that I am here, talking to you in person rather than appearing before millions on television. The problem is an immense one, a hot potato, as we say in politics. We are caught on the horns of a dilemma: if we prevent foreign competition from entering this country we shall have a retaliation against our exporting: if we control the design of shoes, jobs will be lost and dividends will fall. What then is the answer? The answer, good people, lies in education. We must educate the public by exposing the facts; by creating a foot consciousness. Everyone must be made aware of feet. (*Moving back to the table*) Let us hear those facts from the horse's mouth. Doctor, we look to you for information. (*He sits*)
Doctor (*rising*) Thank you, Minister. Of course, in my official capacity, I cannot comment on the malpractices of shoe manu-

facturers or the foolhardiness of the retail trade, that is a
political issue. I can only be concerned with the medical facts,
the stockmarket—sockmarket, and the shoe market is not my
concern. (*He picks up the chart and shows it to the audience. On
it are drawn two feet side by side: the left one has the toes spread
out, but the right one has them bunched together and displays a
huge bunion. He points to the left drawing*) If we compare the
natural foot—(*pointing to the right drawing*)—with a foot which
is the product of bad footwear, we can see at once the result of
the credit squeeze—of squeezing the foot into ill-fitting shoes.
(*He reverses the chart to show a very high-heeled shoe at the top
and an extremely flat shoe at the bottom. Pointing to the top
drawing*) A shoe of this design is likely to affect the bank
balance—the balance of the back, and result in injury to the
spine. (*Pointing at the lower shoe*) Whereas a shoe as flat as this
one is certain to cause fallen dividends,—arches. Ladies and
Gentlemen, I say to you that the feet of our young people are
my investment,—our investment, for a healthy profit,—nation.
My concern is with my shares, I mean, I share your concern, and
will not rest easy until a campaign gives me a rake off—until a
campaign against bad shoes takes off. The facts, I think, speak
for themselves. (*He sits*)

Minister (*standing*) Thank you, Doctor, and thank you, good
people, for coming. You may depend on us to get things
moving. Now, as I have another meeting and the doctor's
patients are waiting, I declare this meeting over.

The Doctor and Minister exit up L

Second Lady (*hobbling across* L, *and shouting after them*) Hum-
bugs! You didn't even try!

Third Lady (*moving to her*) I know that doctor. He treated me
for bunions when I was in my twenties.

First Lady (*moving* R *of the table*) I'm sure the Minister was
sincere, he was trying you know.

Second Lady (*shuffling down* L *and sitting in the downstage chair*)
Let the facts speak for themselves, you call that trying?

Third Lady (*making her way painfully to the chair above the
Second Lady*) Facts never said anything. It's how they're inter-
preted that matters. (*She sits*)

First Lady I expect you're right, dear, I'm very confused. Perhaps we were a little to blame ourselves. I remember you laughing at my school shoes, calling me funny names and . . .

Third Lady (*rising*) So it's our fault now is it?

First Lady No, dear, I didn't mean . . .

Second Lady (*rising*) You had high heels before we did.

Third Lady We looked up to you as a fashion setter.

First Lady Did you really? Well, just fancy, and I thought . . .

Third Lady (*moving down* R *of First Lady*) What if we did put pressure on each other a bit, what really matters is who put the idea in our heads, who set the fashion?

The Shop Steward enters up L

Shop Steward Where's my seat then? I know me rights: a full seat that's what I was promised. Workers' representative I am and don't you forget it!

First Lady Are we in the way?

Shop Steward In the way, you're on the board, ain't yer?

First Lady Board?

Second Lady What Board?

Shop Steward *Steadfast*, I mean, *Withit Shoes* board, of course.

Third Lady No we're not; I wish we had been, that's all. I just wish we had been.

Shop Steward If you're not on the board, you'd better scarper or she'll 'ave you for trespass.

Second Lady (*moving down* R *of the Third Lady*) Come on girls, don't let it ever be said we mixed with this lot.

Third Lady We should stay, tell the truth.

First Lady (*to the Shop Steward*) Well, I'm glad you'll be able to put our point of view; we're glad you're representing the ordinary people.

Shop Steward That's me, Mrs, your representative.

First Lady You'll stop it won't you?

Shop Steward Stop anything, if I don't like it; if it 'arms the workers.

First Lady So *Loppies* will never be made, will they?

Shop Steward Now, just a minute, you listen: *Loppies* is our salvation. Whose side are you on? Wivout *Loppies* this factory's going to close. *Loppies* is different and shoes what is different sells. No *Loppies*, no job. Get it?

First Lady I don't think you understand.

Third Lady (*pulling her across to her seat*) Come and sit down, dear, you're wasting your time.

Second Lady (*hobbling to her old seat*) He'll never see it our way.

First Lady I suppose not. Of course, he is concerned for the workers, I see that.

Shop Steward You've got it, Mrs, that's who I represent, the people.

Miss Less strides in and takes her place at the table. The Shop Steward cringes and backs away

Miss Less (*looking up and seeing the Shop Steward*) Ah, early, that's unusual. Chairs!

Shop Steward Chairs?

Miss Less Chairs, man! You're not stupid are you?

Shop Steward Here, it's not my place! I'm a full member . . .

Miss Less We can't have a meeting without chairs can we now? Two more chairs, please!

Shop Steward (*going off down* R) All right, but I'll bring it up wiv the executive, you see if I don't.

The Shop Steward exits down R. *The Head of Advertising enters up* L.

Head of Advertising I'm not late am I? What a day it's been!

Miss Less No but the others are running it fine. (*Pointing to the chair down* L) Sit there!

The Head of Advertising creeps to the chair down L

Have you screened the *Semi-Spheres* ad. yet?

Head of Advertising Goes out tonight, Madam Chairman.

Miss Less Good, just as well it was delayed since *Withit Shoes* only came into being today. Did you know that?

Head of Advertising Er, no, I had assumed . . .

Miss Less So did I, that's why I commissioned it.

Head of Advertising But the product does exist? I mean . . .

Miss Less It will. Always make things hard to get, that's my motto. Makes them more desirable—you can charge more.

The Minister of Health and the Doctor enter, both are wearing "Loppies", and they lean against each other for support

Minister I'm getting the hang of them, I believe.

Doctor I can't wait to sit down, all the same.

Minister (*to Miss Less*) Little publicity stunt. Monique had them specially made for us.

Doctor Stupid photographer, tilted his camera—completely spoilt the effect.

Miss Less Very commendable, I'm sure, but you should have done our walking course first. Kindly consult me before you try any further stunts.

The Shop Steward enters down R *carrying two chairs*

Shop Steward I 'ad to go down three flights of stairs. The union'll 'ave to look at this.

Miss Less indicates to the Shop Steward to put the chairs RC. *He does this, and sits on the one downstage*

Miss Less (*to the Minister*) I intend that we shall set up walking schools up and down the country. Should be a very profitable sideline.

Doctor (*moving to the chair above the Head of Advertising*) Ah, you'll need medical advice for that. Usual consultant's fees, I hope.

Miss Less To be negotiated, Doctor, nothing is usual from now on.

Shop Steward No private negotiating, everthin's got t' be in the open—first principle of the union.

Minister (*sitting on the chair above the Shop Steward*) I think we should call them "Walking Sports Centres"; "Walking Schools" hasn't the right ring about it. Or perhaps G.H.W.C.s, "Government Health Walking Centres". Abbreviations appeal these days.

Head of Advertising They'll be advertised commercially though?

Minister I'll see you get your cut, never fear.

Miss Less (*looking at her watch*) Nine, eight, seven, six—

The Principal Shareholder enters, he too is wearing a pair of "Loppies"; he stops L *of the table*

—five, four, three, two, one. (*Looking at the Principal Shareholder*) Another three seconds and you would have been late.

Principal Shareholder Little surprise—why I'm late. (*He walks*

*round in a circle, finishing facing the Doctor, and sticks out his
feet to display his shoe*) Special favour from Monique. (*Seeing
the Doctor's shoes*) Oh, I see she spreads her favours.

Miss Less Monique should know better. I declare the meeting
open. Sit!

*The Principal Shareholder looks round and then sits above the
Doctor*

This meeting will not be minuted as we are concerned with a
crucial decision. How shall we launch *Loppies*? Ideas?

Doctor (*standing, rubbing his back*) Well, to be honest, I'm having
second thoughts about this design. Of course, I've never actually
worn fashion shoes before—they're so incredibly uncom-
fortable. Now that I've experienced them, my professional
opinion is that they could be bad for the back; could lead to
scoliosis. (*He sits*)

Miss Less If we don't sell them it will certainly lead to bank-
ruptcy.

Principal Shareholder Not sell them, preposterous! Of course we
must sell them.

Minister I see the Doctor's point though; as a Minister it is my
job to see everyone's point. Compromise, that's the answer,
when in doubt, compromise. Now if we sold two pairs at a
time, girls could wear a low left and a high right on one day
and vice versa on the next.

Doctor Ah, yes, a lean to the left for one day, followed by a lean
to the right for one day would be self-correcting—excellent!

Miss Less Mm, but how could be persuade people to buy com-
plimentary pairs?

Principal Shareholder We can't offer two for the price of one.

Shop Steward Too true, we can't. We're not standing for cut-
price goods—leads to cut-price wages.

Minister If we compromised, we could perhaps sell the second
pair at half-price. If it was purchased at the same time.

Miss Less The turnover would have to be high.

Minister Perhaps a government warning, say: "These shoes can
damage your health unless you buy two pairs".

Head of Advertising An ad. on the commercial network would be
more effective.

Miss Less Perhaps we should have Monique in on this. After all, it does affect the design concept. (*To the Shop Steward*) Summon her, will you!

Shop Steward (*rising*) 'Ere, it's not my job.

Miss Less It affects all our jobs.

Shop Steward (*crossing* R *of Miss Less's desk, then turning to her*) Victimization, that's what this is—victimization.

Miss Less (*pointing at the feet of the Doctor and the Minister*) Well, you can't expect them to walk far in those.

The Shop Steward exits up L

Shop Steward (*as he goes, muttering*) Shall inform the executive.

Minister Saw your ad. for *Semi-Spheres* today. Had a preview. Is it quite honest to offer something that doesn't exist? After all, *Withit Shoes* only came into being a few minutes ago.

Principal Shareholder First create your demand, first law of business.

Miss Less We've put *Withit Shoes* on the map. Everyone will be trying to buy a pair. When they don't succeed, they'll think they're scarce because everyone wants them.

Principal Shareholder They'll snap anything up with the *Withit* label after that.

Doctor Frankly, I'm glad *Semi-Spheres* don't exist. Those free crutches worried me. After all, crutches are a medical matter.

Principal Shareholder You don't think we were really going to give free crutches with every pair do you? We're not a philanthropic organization.

Minister I am uneasy about *Semi-Spheres*.

Monique and the Shop Steward enter up L

They could put a strain on the Health Service.

Miss Less Ah, Monique, come and sit here will you. (*She indicates the chair next to herself*)

Monique Madame is too kind.

Shop Steward (*moving to his old chair*) You're dead right! She's not even a full member of the board.

Miss Less Now, Monique, I've had a bright idea. We sell *Loppies* in sets of two pairs, a right-hand lean, together with a left. What do you think?

Head of Advertising It's a cinch for the big ad.

Doctor Justifiable on medical grounds.

Minister It could have government sponsoring.

Shop Steward Make plenty of overtime.

Monique Madame, I 'ave to—'ow you say—speak like Frank.

Shop Steward Drop the phoney accent, gal, everyone here knows you ain't French.

Monique (*to the Shop Steward*) No sense of culture you ain't, an' that's a fact.

Miss Less Well, what do you think?

Monique It stinks!

Miss Less What?

Monique Don't you see what'll 'appen: they'll take the left of one pair wiv the right of the other. Then where'll we be—back to old flatties and platforms.

Miss Less We'll have lost our uniqueness.

Principal Shareholder Our best selling point.

Miss Less Well, ladies, it looks as if Monique has put her finger on an unseen weakness in your little scheme.

Third Lady (*hobbling* R *of Miss Less*) We've heard quite enough.

Second Lady (*limping down* R) More than enough.

First Lady (*shuffling, holding her back, up* L *of the Third Lady*) I'm afraid I have to agree.

Miss Less Who are you?

Third Lady You're used to models and demonstrations—let's see how you like this one. (*She totters in a circle, leaning heavily on her stick*)

Second Lady Here we have Jean, with the unique Monique ankles. Notice the graceful movement and elegant stick. Only *Withit* shoes can give you pleasure like this.

The Third Lady stops down R, *leaning heavily on her stick. The second Lady drags the First Lady* C, *then performs to the Head of Advertising*

Second Lady A short commercial break. (*To the First Lady*) You poor darling, fancy having to go through life with such normal feet.

First Lady (*holding her back*) I have my back to comfort me.

Second Lady I envy you your back. How did you acquire it?

First Lady I envy you your bunions. How did you get them?

Second Lady I have *Withit Shoes* to thank.

First Lady I have *Withit Shoes* to thank.

Second Lady How lucky we met.
First Lady (*to the audience*) Now we can have the worst of all possible worlds.

The Third Lady joins them

First Lady
Second Lady } For a without it world tomorrow } (*Singing
Third Lady } Get *Withit Shoes* today. } *together*)

They link arms and dance down R

Head of Advertising (*standing*) I accept no responsibility. The product is no concern of mine. (*He sits*)
Minister (*standing*) The government is blameless, we cannot suppress private initiative. (*He sits*)
Principal Shareholder (*standing*) I'm concerned only with return on capital. (*He points at Miss Less*) The product is her concern. (*He sits*)
Miss Less (*standing*) I only make what you buy.
Monique (*standing*) I only design what you demand.

Monique and Miss Less sit

Doctor (*standing*) We can only advise; we cannot control. (*He sits*)
Shop Steward (*standing*) You only stop manipulation through organization. Speak as one brothers, speak as one. (*He sits*)

They all freeze, except the Three Ladies

Third Lady I blame Mother.
Second Lady I blame advertising.
Third Lady 1 blame the manufacturers.
Second Lady The designer.
Third Lady The shopkeeper.
Second Lady The doctors.
Third Lady The government.
First Lady Who knows, dears, perhaps it's just human nature that's to blame. (*Looking all round*) I'm sure we'll all be very happy here when we get used to it. (*Facing the Second and Third ladies*) We musn't dwell in the past, no good ever came of that.

CURTAIN

FURNITURE AND PROPERTY LIST

On stage: 6 futuristic chairs
Off stage: Several boxes of shoes (**Shop Assistant**)
     Clapperboard (**Television Director**)
     Earphones, camera, tripod (**Cameraman**)
     Wand (**Fairy Godmother**)
     Pair of "semi-sphere" shoes (**Fairy Godmother**)
     Pair of crutches (**Fairy Godmother**)
     Small table, papers (**White-Coated Women**)
     2 chairs (**White-Coated Women**)
     Loppie shoes (**Monique**)
     Chart (**Doctor**)
     Loppie shoes (**Minister of Health**)
     Loppie shoes (**Doctor**)
     Loppie shoes (**Principal Shareholder**)
     2 chairs (**Shop Steward**)
Personal: **Mother:** handbag with £5 notes

LIGHTING PLOT

Property fittings required: nil
Interior. A day room
No cues

MADE AND PRINTED IN GREAT BRITAIN BY
LATIMER TREND & COMPANY LTD PLYMOUTH

MADE IN ENGLAND